CHAOTIC MUSINGS

"Five minute limit"

VIBE UNION

Lots of people

Acknowledgement

We would like to acknowledge the true custodians of the land on which Radio Talk takes place, the Woiwurrung and Boonwurrung people of the Kulin Nation.

We acknowledge that treaties have never been signed and sovereignty was never ceded. We cannot change the past so we must understand the negative impact that colonisation has had upon the First Nations people.

It is important to understand and recognise that we at Vibe Union are lucky and privileged to put on an open mic every two weeks, where people are able to express themselves and tell their stories. First Nations people in Australia have had their voices silenced and their stories untold throughout history, continuing to this present day.

As the MC of Radio Talk I would also like to acknowledge the Palawa people of Lutruwita where I was born and raised in Tasmania.

CHAOTIC MUSINGS

Preface

Hello everyone, this is Jason, your poetic MC and alongside me on this adventure is the trusty sound engineer, Ry.

Let's get some sexy admin out of the way so you can enjoy the actual poetry.

Vibe Union started creating this chaotic poetry community, beginning in 2021, under the name of 'Talking Blue' renaming to 'Radio Talk' after a year or so.

We have continued to thrive as a night where things are occasionally unpredictable and mainly chaotic, but ultimately, a cathartic space of expression for many different types of poetry.

Despite a particular world event that shall not be named, Radio Talk has been Melbourne's most consistent open mic poetry since we began. Persisting into online spaces due to lockdowns, making sure we continued our event for people to express themselves. To this day, we have never missed a night and we are proud of this fact.

This book celebrates the journey so far of the amazing poetry community here in Melbourne. There was little debate over the creation of this book, honouring those who come along and support Vibe Union.

Contents

Acknowledgement   iii
Preface   vii

Jason (MC) - Dopamine   1
Ry Wood - A Queer Whore Story   4
Amutha - Hurry Up & slo w d o w n   7
Gerard - Paint Me an Apocalypse   9
Izzy (last name redacted) - Broken Wings   11
Jocelyn - Wicked Men   14
Antonio - War Machine   15
Xlvi Joon - Tonight   18
S.T.P - That Sounds Exhausting   20
Saskia McKippers - The Stoic Obsession with Figs   23
Kelsey Jean - You've Changed   25
Lane Milburn - Good Morning   26

Michael Bromberg - The Sous-Chef and the Fish (A Culinary Affair)	28
Daniel Whimpey - Charli, Charli, Charli	30
Jaidyn L Attard - The Beatnik	32
Rhath - Alone, Finally	34
Beverley - Vibe Union	36
Marcus Graham - Still	38
Jett - Commentary Rendition (AFL)	40
Raphael - Fire on the Sand	42
Matcho - Passion	44
Milky Bar Kid - The Cycle	46
Shyaire Ganglani - Wigbolt	47
Nayomi Senanayake - Home Pt II	48
Amy - Fuck You Helen	50
Thank You	53

Jason (MC) - Dopamine

I like to drink wine at 10am, doom scrolling on my phone simultaneously watching two different shows on separate screens paying no attention to any of them

It's red wine, it's healthy
All hyperbolic of course

I go to therapy
Meaning:
I watch people ten years younger on TikTok describing my diagnoses in more details than anyone ever has

What other choice do I have?
I went to my GP to get a psych referral
Their response: Good luck
Challenge accepted
Psyches "aren't taking new patients" so I lost mine

So why not drink red wine at 10am, doom scrolling on my phone simultaneously watching two different shows on separate screens paying no attention to any of them

Don't I have a job to go to?
I worked for myself, independently, supporting a young man with schizophrenia and autism

Eventually, three days a week I would have the shit beaten out of me
He once asked me how old SpongeBob was, I said 15, like you, bad decision
I was lucky when he came back from the kitchen he only had a spatula
Not a knife

Maybe I should see a professional about that trauma
Oh wait, not taking new patients
Good luck

So why not drink red wine at 10am, doom scrolling on my phone, simultaneously watching two different shows on separate screens paying no attention to any of the them

I will never be able to own a home, although afforded the right to pay rent that costs more than mortgage payments but unemployment doesn't allow that to happen because what if I couldn't pay the bank?

It's okay to be fucked over by greedy landlords who care not for the wellbeing of the renters
Requiring payments to survive harsh times of rising inflation, my heart breaks for their passive income and lack of sympathy, they are the true battlers
I should feel honoured they do the bare fucking minimum, expecting to be treated like the Saints of housing

So why not drink red wine at 10am, doom scrolling on my phone simultaneously watching two different shows on separate screens paying no attention to any of the the

Feeling helpless watching the rise of evangelical Christianity and neo-Nazis marching with police protection because they're scared of drag queens reading to children in fear of grooming
Staying silent about pastors, priests and youth group leaders, statistically more likely to abuse children

And continue to do so

Trying to eradicate trans people for merely existing, stating how autism is linked to gender diversity which is true, so guess what? They'll come for neurodiversity next

So why not drink red wine at 10am, doom strolling on my phone simultaneously watching two different shows on separate screens paying no attention to any of the them

Listening to thoughts and prayers
By those creating these nightmares

It's not the blood of jesus I have in my cup, instead the tears he should be shedding for how bad he fucked this world up
I still want to give thanks to god though, for making me autistic, so I never have to believe in him again

@user.name.unknown.jason

Ry Wood - A Queer Whore Story

Fuck these genial queers I'm busting genitals here,
I bringing boys back from the bath house cuz I left my baseball bat at the crack house
And the blast houses 9s but I ain't a bloodlettin bitch
I'd rather collect with a threat than escalate that violence.
S'why I call Cammy when I'm feelin' they scammed me
Cuz I tell folks I'm a pacifist, it's a polite way to own up
That I'm a coward who's afraid of their demons when they show up.
And I know my mates prefer to blow up more than me,
So I get back to working corners till I'm the name on the street.

Gettin' lost in the sauce, call the big man boss.
Lemme be your rag, baby gimme a toss.
I need real rough shit from a real big dick.
Gotta bottle of crisco, write my name on ya wrist
I want a hate fuck, i ain't gonna tuck
I'm a powerbottom like the Babadook.
Gonna tie me up like Penelope Pitstop;
Like a Ringling Thing, centre stage on a Big Top.
I'mma 3 Ring actor better know what to ask for.
If you Netflix n' Chill, better save it for next door.
Here we're Amsterdam, Sir you gonna need a day planner
So once the Tour Bus' stopping, reckon I'mma need an answer.

Ass like toast, cuz the dick gets jammed;
Cheeks like butter when I spread 'em cross you man.
Call that backside an Oreo; stuffed with creme
When you're washing down my milk, call this bitch a Dairy Queen.
Man's colon lookin' like punched eclair,
Earned that P.H.D., pretty hefty derriere.
Got 'em pounding out his cock-toral thesis
Need hoe library when I'm checkin all these dicks
Wanna they/them pussy check my I.S.B.N,
I'm way at the back top shelf non-fiction,
Fuckin your mans on the Big Book O' Medicine
Category: Cunt - Class One Addiction.

Reckon I'mma fuck a whole congregation,
Got your balls like a Bishop, at your confirmation
Drainin my sac when they rubbin my prostate
Busting my tapes like they catching me at Watergate
Got a hose 'o Holy Water; ready to coat 'em,
Givin' out commandments like I wrote 'em;
Thou shan't spit when you suckin' this totem,
Begging for the blessin'?
- "In Nomine Padre" -
Unfillin' my Scrotum.

I'm making dollars spinnin' dick, you can call me Lil' Vader,
Told 'em, "That's a good Trick!" Then we went again later.
When the spot's too hot, drop me like a grand pian'na.
If the keys don't sing then I play the sledge hammer.

Did a split on that dick, calling me gym-nasty.
Swallowed a load of his kids, I'll be ending a dynasty.
Doing tricks on my clit, blew it like plastique.
Sissy fuss, lift him up, till he bust-up on my Sinner's Peak
Score every night with the team,
Call that the winner's league.
Pussy gonna drip, get a plumber cuz we gotta leak.
Work him up until I get paid, calling me an industry,

Thicker than my hips, gonna call that cum a milkshake.
Your man's gave their best, the rest was brief.
Took my pound in flesh on the sheets, pausing my head to scream.
Their senses leave, my hair's the reins,
Their neck's my sleeve.
I text my team, flood 'em in the sex, "sleep tight; wet dreams."
Come the morning next feeling light in my knees.
When I cashed his check to pay the rent,
Next week I'm gonna do it all again, but please don't tell the police.

@BBaeScribbles

Amutha - Hurry Up & slo w d o w n

I've got some advice for you
It gets easier

But then it gets harder
again*

Because life
just
does
that

And maybe advice is more for the
g i v e r
rather than the receiver

I want to
[decompress]
but this
< i n e r t i a >
is collapsing us with full force

So, I better love it
Or at least learn to

I might forget just how
f r ee i n g
it is to let g.... o

Keep finding myself back at the
door
S
T
E
P
of presence

Knocking for
eternity | ytinrete

Until I let myself
back
in

----
*a long ass time

@amutha.vibes

Gerard - Paint Me an Apocalypse

From a leftover crackerjack
I'll pluck a crêpe-paper crown
and hereupon will I name myself
Esteemed Lord of Come-What-May.
I'll employ some unknown halfwit,
a subject of little renown,

whose hands are yet imbued
with artistry sans peril
to paint my perilous mansion
on its parched and barren estate,
but somehow to erase the misery
that howls from wall and rafter;
to brush-smooth every wrinkle
of my mausoleum features,
to fake the glint of nobility
in each hard-boiled, bloodshot eye,
to uncover uncut diamonds
from under my bastard skin.
I will find me such a fool
on the outskirts of Destiny,
perched and piss-sodden drunk,
singing ditties of hayloft pussy

on some slate-tiled tavern roof;
I'll groom him and commission
a colossal trompe-l'oeil painting,
an illusion of a gaping abyss
that could swallow my loveless world.

Izzy (last name redacted) - Broken Wings

I cannot mend these broken wings
with stapler, tape, clips and things
I am the bird that no longer sings
The hope I once held, I no longer bring

I am the seamstress who weeps in the night
Worn out, burnt out, snuffed out
like a light

I cannot mend these broken wings
nor restore the crowns of queens and kings
Lies that tarnish burnished rings
Omissions wound like insect stings

"Stop caring", they say
"Put yourself first"
And suffer as I watch them?
Tell me which is worse?
You heard it here first,
empathy is a curse

I cannot mend these broken wings
My metronomic mood swings

Irritability increases and like ivy, it clings
If you drown me, no one wins

Waves of rage, tsunami of panic
Constant anxiety, holding together your Titanic
I'm shell, I'm husk, I'm empty
Tympanic

I cannot mend these broken wings
Light refracts from shards long splintered
Chaos that was never mine
yet it is I, it seems,
who is always hindered

And sorry is just a word,
Sorry is just a WORD
Your inaction, distraction, delayed reaction
My dim-witted faith in your no plans of action

I cannot mend these broken wings
You dance with devils, have with demons
your flings
Does no one care for me to prosper?
A peaceful life I must try to foster

Why is it your wish for me to watch you perish?
Heart, sweat, blood and tears
I've given to all of whom I've cherished

I cannot mend these broken wings
I have to cut these apron strings!
I know you're set on ending things
but my wellbeing is not your plaything!

I'm too dogged to walk away
Another apology and I'll stay
Tell me again how it will all be okay

because if I fold, there will be hell to pay

I cannot mend these broken wings
So please! Stop bringing them to me!
I'm slowly dropping the plates I carry
I'm losing myself, can't you see?

Open your eyes!
But even open, you're too blinded to see
that bearing your burdens is destroying me
Taking advantage of my good nature,
my softness, my honesty
I leave behind my legacy of charity

I cannot mend these broken wings
My knuckles white, I am slipping
Grit my teeth and with all my might,
overlook the reciprocity that's missing

Broken people with pretty broken wings
Patched with tape and bound with string
Whether acquaintance, friend, foe or kin
It's high time I save my own skin

@littleizzyruth

Jocelyn - Wicked Men

If I could gather all the wicked men from history,

I would set them down together

To taste the tantalizing salt of power,

Flavouring each ego.

With burnt eyes of fire,

Addicted, to repeatedly bleed

Not quite to death on unfulfilled desires.

@joc1_23

Antonio - War Machine

I can't see past the people with credit card smiles
& no outlines, a blur of fast haircuts
I'm honoured to be on borrowed time
the devil's debt
Melbourne will kill me
leave pieces of me scattered through bars
on tables lying next to old pieces of paper
a life made of clean pages & filthy ink
dressed in brass knuckles & red lipstick

I've spent whole days drowning in mother nature's warmth of mirrors
clinging to evolution's chipped tooth, screaming, repeating the questions, getting
different answers & all of them are lies

how many did you believe?

the light left streak marks on the glass
casting a shadow that will later be outlined
drop dead gorgeous
I've been lucky enough to bury friends
one day I'll grant my people the same privilege

I wasn't born of the body of a woman
I was sent to kill kings
indulging in the fascination of paid-for freedom
I've never looked as good as I have in this room with you
the warm glow of gas lighting, it's flattering

the unfocused haze of dreaming settled in the hallway
making escape feel as unrealistic as ghosts
being self-assured to be unnerving
looking through fingers seeing the bars that separate us

the night on your cheekbones hurts the most
sitting at the defendant's table
in front of a judge baptized in the black robes of saints
adorned by pressed wax halos
playing coerced confessions
of police negligence
I'm at the defendant's table bathed in green neon light
accuser's pointing to identify me
index fingers reaching, gnawing at the air that separates us
pulling to reach further than the arm of justice will allow
we're all in on the joke
it's comforting
we love to glorify the past
plan for tomorrow
& wait for the day to end
feeling morose with marks of the stigmata
thanks to tiktok the revolution will be televised
hidden in back pockets
locked behind screens
I'm a cog in the machine of AmeriKKKas dirty dream
I am
have been
iron man's
right hand
man

I am
a war machine

@antoniomontaine

Xlvi Joon - Tonight

I stand before you, my dear friends at our usual open mic
as a woman that pretends to be composed and calm alike
when this is certainly not true - I hold ample to confess
as there is something I must do to pull myself out of a mess.
First of all, the trying bid for me to do the honourable
announce that I present new shit to reveal myself most vulnerable.
My daughter is away on camp so I can get away with swearing
and details blasted through the amp that else would be too daring.
Previously I too have hidden behind this paper and these lines
in self-consciousness forbidden to share the darkness in my mind.

Tonight my heart speaks out instead and intends to let you know
the sorrow troubling my head as there's someplace I have to go.
My past has mostly served me well yet left me living life in hope.
Like Madonna, I live to tell that deception ends the rope.
A man that I have made time for has received my true affection
became the one I would adore quietly in self-protection.
Fearful avoidant that's my style, not something I announce with
pride

I kept my heart closed for a while as not to show my vulnerable side.
Cautious to avoid what hurts and naturally I'm now twice shy
I hide behind vagueness of words without the intent of a lie
but what's the point in forming rhyme to avoid a truth and dare
if I cannot speak up in time to make the other one aware.

As this is something quite unfair I explored beyond my shadow
and showed how much I deeply cared - he didn't do the same at all.
Every other thing came first; clever words kept me at bay
what would confuse me even worse: those clever words that made me
stay.

Like a puppet on a string he had me here there everywhere
to accommodate his whim, stop me from going anywhere.
Tonight I have someplace to be even though it makes me nervous
to preserve my dignity and release what doesn't serve us.
Too many days I hoped for texts that would confirm to me I
mattered;

Too many nights turned into sex without the deep affection added.
Two seasons had gone by like that but after daylight savings
I have wondered where we're at with how we've been behaving.
I'm not comfortable with worry, not fond of second guessing
although I am not in a hurry, the lack of clarity is stressing.
My feelings have been kept on hold as confusion served him well.
My take on it I haven't told, now gathered strength enough to tell.
He's expecting me tonight but has no clue what I will say
I'm not preparing for a fight just reveal my thoughts today.
To most this must sound so pathetic but to me a massive step
to prompt a talk that's not synthetic and address all that's been kept.
Thank you for being this safe space for me and others to confide in
besides the pain my saving grace to accept me out of hiding.

S.T.P - That Sounds Exhausting

Do you mind listening for a while?
Could you just take this weight
For a minute?
Or an extended minute?
Because i'm a combination of feeling like a mouse on a round wheel
running thing
And a tennis ball on a tandem pole
Yoyoing back and forth
Between total control
And complete despair
This isn't a cry for help
Though the few tears i shed today
Certainly helped
It's an exercise in
if i keep saying how i feel
I might hear myself
And i might actually listen

I remember telling someone
About having anxiety
Explaining this highly strung
Mindset
They responded with

"Fuck that sounds exhausting"
This state of questioning
This state of self belief
This state autopilot
Are we hard on ourselves
Fuck yeah
Could we do better
Sure

This is some unedited
Lacking in perfectionism
Ramblings
In Trying to find some solace and stillness in this current time of my life

I started doing the work years ago
Only to realise
It's a never ending Job

I keep talking
And the more i talk
The less i understand
The less i feel i know
But deep down i also know that's not true

I know if i came back next radio talk
I could speak some self loving
Uplifting
How good are things poem
But right now
That's not me

This sludge is thick
And the laces on my boots aren't coping
But i have boots
I have determination
And surely this sludge is sitting on a hill

That i'm almost at the top of
The uphill battle
Is getting shorter with every step

But i'm also just a little mouse who would like
To stop running for a while

@s.t.p_s.t.p

Saskia McKippers - The Stoic Obsession with Figs

You follow prophecies of enlightenment etched into stone guiding
eyes to answers that you desired but couldn't find,
A racing heart shadowing red twines that instruct you of the virtues
of bliss;
Weaved ties of grapevines you trace in your palms, the laugh lines
forming around his lips;
You both track the fig trees which surround the home acquired with
key rings on finger tips entwined in cupped hands.

You coconspire in whispers at the deli nearing the end of your street;
Softly wonder which soft cheeses pair well with the ripening days of
Autumn,
Light dapples across full cheeks stained in waxy hues,
The perfect rinds that cover branches beckoning you nearer,
The sagging mould encircles the weight of swelling fruits;
You love each other black and blue,
Eyes and mouths wrinkling, hands tingling with eagerness to take
hold of opened flesh.
You make prayers to classical gods at the roots of their temples;
Deities for love, for tranquillity, for abundance-

Throats filled with the wine he pours into your cup;
something red, something bold,
Something to soften your spine into the shrine you have unearthed.

You find joy in the mornings spent jointly mapping the fig trees that continue to ripen,
Leaving the firm green fruits to soften while at laborious shifts spent watching nights pass through stained glass, neon lights staggering to bed come to the arriving dawn;
Sunday was spent in repent on knees beside fellow disciples of the comfort you build;
laughter bubbling in the backs of throats to wash away with fermented honey,
rolling plastic faith between fingers for powdered blessings;
You provide for the soil you have chosen to cultivate; ripping out the weeds of decay burrowed deep within you; a wasp sting within the bud of your chest;
How the death of yourself has formed into this.
Your dogma of loneliness matures into the fertile earth for tenderness to germinate.
What you come to understand is how you've begun to draw lines towards the ways you've developed a taste for happiness; how it wraps around the pit of your belly to fill your body with sweetness.

You count down the days until April arrives and labour begins;
pulling at bare twigs, you harvest the stoic teachings.
You imagine yourself climbing to the canopy as you did as a child;
once in escape, you suppose, from what remained below on mortal lands.
He waits beneath the fig leaves,
Palms up, hands open, waiting for you to drop sticky parts of you into his grasp.
And you will do so, willingly.
When the harvest is done,
you receive the space between your ribs where he sows new seeds.

@chaupaemisque

Kelsey Jean - You've Changed

I don't call it changing,
I'm just becoming more myself.
There was so much fear and hatred in those words,
"You've changed"
A sense of finality
An unwillingness to acknowledge
This new knowledge of mine
Something I had always known,
Now finding space to grow
That acorn tree beckoning me
To grow higher, and fuller
To reach further for the sunshine
While roots reached further into the earth
Holding myself steady,
A solid foundation
On which to build
Forever growing, and learning, and... changing
But I don't call it changing
I'm just becoming more myself

@kelseyjean_is

Lane Milburn - Good Morning

If you want to make an omelette, you've gotta break a few eggs, right?
But there is comfort in control, I eat the same thing for breakfast as I do for dinner at night.
Eggs on toast and eggs on toast and eggs on toast on toast on toast on toast on toast.
I don't trust the gas and the flame so I try not to cook them on the pan over the stove.
I microwave them, for 42 seconds, eggsactly.
And the bread has to be toasted somewhere between the html colours coded #e9d4b7 and #ddbe91 to be satisfactory.
I do 12 pushups every morning, and then I do 26 squats. I plank for 33 seconds, brush my teeth twice. I floss. 3 shots of coffee and 30 minutes of reading, I pick at my face until my skin starts bleeding, take photos of my head to track my hairline receding, practice my lines in the mirror until I'm confident in speaking.
Good morning. Good morning. Good morning. Good morning. It never sounds right the first time, when I speak, words taste like they've expired, I have to repeat them over and over until they've lost all their meaning and it's just echoes and syllables of other people's language that I've acquired.
I watch the same movie more than once, and when I read books I read them cover to cover, then I read them back to front.

But, you should reserve some things just for special occasions so they don't lose their specialness. So a painting doesn't turn dimensionless, a dress that stopped feeling elegant, press play for endless prevalence of songs that just turned into, resonance.

I used to have a lot of trouble sleeping so I'd always watch the sunrise just to make sure it still came up every day. I figured I'd never get bored of it because a sunrise never shows it's colours twice in the same way.

Just because it repeats, it's reliable but it doesn't mean that it's not still moveable.

You can have too much of a good thing. You don't need to be an addict to build a tolerance to something beautiful.

Good morning. Good morning. Good morning. Good morning. I used to watch the sunrise. Now I just watch the day stop being night.

@lunarlane

Michael Bromberg - The Sous-Chef and the Fish (A Culinary Affair)

The sous-chef looking at the fish
gets lost within its cloudy eye
remembers not the salty dish
forgets the who the how the why.
he looks into that iris grey
which wetly brims with mortal pain
is crying out, is crying out, alack alack, in vain in vain
the young man looks round in dismay
but no one else is watching.
the sous-chef sees that bloodless lip
which plunged deep with a sharp hookd kiss
had lusted for the flesh of shrimp
les (forbidden) fruits de mer.
so thrashing on that old swart ship
he felt the Wrath of God.
so writhing on that whetted tip
the bloodied Hand of God.
i screamed into the great abyss, into that broiling sea *what good to me*
Eternal Bliss?
oh Lord, don't let it come to this!

i've erred, by Jove, it isn't fair
at least let me repent.
now who shall wish my wife goodnight?
now who shall raise my children right?
'gainst the rotting boards of a rotting hull, he wildly beat his fishy skull forget Your damned Eternal Life!
just give me just one more day of this, Oh God, Dear God just one more day! and then
i'll gladly swim into perdition, yes
oh let me see the stars once more
and once my daughters as before
then Satan with his wicked paw
can do as he sees fit.
the sous-chef gasps with great surprise
tears welling in his fishy eyes
despair goes swelling in his breast
and crushing now his heaving chest.
the head-chef sees her man go limp
she rushes to his side
she wipes his clammy brow to kiss
his wet unseeing eyes
she plants on him a briny kiss
and to revive me strives.

Juliet

Yea, noise? Then I'll be brief. O, happy dagger,
This is thy sheath. There rust, and let me die.

Exeunt.

@usermb17

Daniel Whimpey - Charli, Charli, Charli

Dear my little princess, my whittle muffin,

Oh Charli, Charli, Charli brown.
Do you hear me, do you hear my sound.
My little princess, with your shiney crown, always a grin never to frown.

Why did Charli, get gnarly, lost the plot.
Oh Charli, Charli, Charli brown.
I'm sorry for he, protected his mum.
Why didn't you hear me, why didn't you listen to me.
I hate myself, but we would of lost more but you're my core.
Life without you is a chore, how I miss the touch of your paw.

My poor Charli, Charli, Charli brown.
Always do I love you, always do I hear your sound.
My little princess, my little boxing machine, you made life supreme.

How much I wish, I wish, I wish, you listened to me, Charli brown.
My special little angel, now your with my best.
I'll miss you, just as much as I do the rest.
How we use to sleep, so tight, close to each other.
How close you'd get, I'd call you a clinger, while you try to smother.

Oh Charli, Charli, Charli brown.
I can hear you, I can hear your sound.
My little princess, you forever wear your crown, always smiling never had a frown.

Our love will never get lost, in my heart, it will always be found.
Charli, remember when you jumped out, you tried to chase me, you ended up in the pound.
I'll always remember your smile, I'll always remember your face.
The love we shared, something from above, that special faith.

Oh Charli, Charli, Charli brown.
I can hear you, I can hear your sound.
My little princess, in my heart you will always be found.

May you rest in peace my beautiful muffin, fuck how life is the biggest mystery, proving to be nothing but the fucking hardest misery.
But princess, I promise, I'll win.

I'll re write history, I love you. Please be looking down with a grin.
Like as we said goodbye, I told you I love Charli, I love you Charli, I love you Charli. I fucking love you Charli.

P.s. Never, ever would I forget your beautiful soul, oh and I loved you had a double chin.

@gingersthetics

Jaidyn L Attard - The Beatnik

Journal on lap on the Flinders stairs
smudging the ink on the lined page,
filling rapid with words like I don't care
there's no time for a grammar rage —

A shadow drops onto my crouched body
and pulls me up from my little book,
she looks like Patti Smith copied,
not a detail I know how to overlook.

She tips her hat and sweeps her hair
like long black seaweed in a curtain,
asks me why I'm writing there
and peers down into my journal.

I tell the beatnik why I write
on the city streets like a vagabond,
murmur what I'm writing about tonight
and she looks at me like she's God.

'You write about such awful things,'
she says as if I didn't already know,
'Why not write about butterfly wings?
The stranger tales aren't yours though.'

The beatnik can think that if she will
but I lived the cold hard truth myself,
there's just no reason for me to spill
the story of my life off the bloody shelf

@jaidynpoetry

Rhath - Alone, Finally

"Alone, finally" they screamed.

With seals clasping shut,
with echoes dying,
with dust settling,
with memories fading,
they sighed with relief.

"Alone, finally" they said,
watching the first moment carefully
as it seemed to stretch on forever.

First, the rhythm fell.
Beats and counters slowed to clutter
while melodies transposed into
haunting underscores of worry.
Scents drifted away next.
The smell of heat and company cooled
as it stagnated and turned.
Then dissipated the murmurs and laughter.
Shouts of cheer and raucous approval
translated quickly into loops and repetitions
of insanity and fear.

"Alone, finally" they whispered.

Their eyes watched the closing gap.
Their hearts ceased pulsing.

Then the light faded.

"Finally" they wept.

What came next was nothing.

@rhath_music

Beverley - Vibe Union

Once there were Poets who know it,
Know they needed to go out and show it,
Show us that we definitely could do it,
Writing and being on stage we did it.
There was tall Jason and his Akubra,
Being the MC on stage and the best by far,
Ry and his mixing producing skills are the best,
His energy and enthusiasm shows no rest,
Kelsey has so much flair and dare with lots of care,
She croons on her guitar, soft as a teddy bear.
DillyDave the Milky Bar kid loves his rap,
Poetry, Rap and his beloved peak cap,
Dave loves to write songs and create,
Create, dream and radiate,
Dave and Jason love their beards,
Hair and brains have them steered,
Steered to entertain us for years,
Motivate and make us laugh until tears.
Amutha with her outfits to surprise,
Her singing and writing talents as bright as a sunrise,
Samuel comes and goes and can talk a lot,
Making us laugh and ponder at a trot,
Nick the hot guitarist is gifted as can be,
His instruments as groovy like you and me,
Huich and her violin are as close as can be,

Her extraordinary talents you need to see,
Saskia with her beautiful camera is a star,
Saskia and her photos have raised the bar.
A smokin hot poetry night is the result,
Of so much creative works no doubt,
Thoughts and actions have come together,
Creating Talking Blue, let's shake the feather.
Talking Blue is a night of love,
Love for human beings and above.
Nights for cares and being soft as a dove.
Here's to another year of poems and lyrics,
Best by far is that there are no gimmicks.
Insta and FB are showing us to the world,
Poetry is here, Vibe Union is unfurled!

@sparklingms.b

Marcus Graham - Still

She is light on her feet, always on the move.
Better catch up.
Cause a girl like that can pass you in a second and she will not look back.
When someone comes running by like that, you suddenly feel so...

Still.

It can seem we're behind, when we look so far ahead.
Thought I was running all this time, won't get far if you don't know where to head.

Do you really want her? Does she really want you?
Then why are you still here?
Cause here's what I know, here feels safe, because here is what I know,
here's where the days move slow,
here's where the wind don't blow,
here's where your seeds won't grow,
But you are not stuck, there is a place we all have to go.

She moves as fast as light,
If you can keep her pace, you may find a place in that glow from her eyes.
So I run, I run like my home's caught fire.

Truth is, I'm so tired. All the time.
I want her to be still, just for a moment.
So we can catch our breath, but instead I hold it.
Are you still there? Were you ever here?

Well I'm here now, here I am, waiting to be there with you.
Why am I always falling or flying, can't I step back and enjoy the view?
Because whether you're high in the sky, or left high and dry,
is all relative to who's eyes you look through.

If you look far ahead, there's always a twinkle on the horizon,
sometimes to find it, you need some assistance
However the same is true when you look too far behind,
Sometimes it's hard to tell the difference.
Is she ahead in the distance? She's running this way.
What are you running towards? Or are you running away?
Did you always have to run that way?
When I see how hard she's running, I can't help but run too.
This day will not be here forever, this home, these places.
The wind will eventually turn on you, everything changes.
Yet we move on, we keep on moving, plant new seeds, turn new pages.

We run. Because against all odds, we are still here.
And just like that, we pass through each other like a flash of light
through a polaroid and for a moment.

She feels still, so still,
And the only sound I hear in my head,
Is her breath in my ear,
and you're there.

@mgproductions2007

Jett - Commentary Rendition (AFL)

So here we are, at the MCG, with a great game of footy, its about to be. Two top 8 teams, looking rather dominant, Petracca in the midfield, Dusty the Equivalent. The siren sounds, with a mid centre bounce, Gawny in the ruck, with the power to renounce. Through the corridor they go, with a formation of flow, delivered inside fifty, this ain't their first rodeo.

With two goals in quick succession, they're firing up, with all the possession. The immediate transfer, with all motion, Richmond are hungry, to make a home ground impression. Bolton with spoil, makes his opponents blood boil, so he takes off down the wing, leaving Melbourne in turmoil. All eyes on the target, with a chip towards the pocket, who's the big fella receiving? Check the Sportsbet market.

Lynch, off the outside of his boot, in career best form, he'll always constitute. With a patient build up again from Richmond, they're starting to stick a few early tonight, as we now watch them converge on the footy, the G reads a hundred degrees Fahrenheit. But they can't afford to get too cocky, here comes Oliver, ready to speccy. He takes the mark and leaves Nankervis to bark, he wanted the free, but he's missed the ballpark.

Brayshaw with the bust up, sends it on his way, Richmond still have numbers, watch the footy ricochet. Cochin somehow rips it out of congestion, the former captain, with one intention. From fifty metres out, its gotta come back, they hustle and bustle deep, its our main man Jack! The score is sixty a piece, late in the term, Benny Brown kicks another, which is quite a concern.

A little fumble from Turner, creates an overlap, picked up by Rioli, with a right foot snap! Dodging and weaving through traffic, Melbourne's form, now a bit sporadic. Weiderman launches a penetrating kick, geeze he's a good young kid, but very optimistic. With an empty goal square, who the fuck is there? One bounce, two bounce, the players unaware.

With three mins twenty, of game play to go, with under one goal down, where's the maestro? Petracca under pressure, trying to recall, the ref blows the whistle, holding the ball! Here comes Dusty, from half forward flank, the Tigers fans know, he's got more in the tank. With only one man capable, of going the distance, he wins the game for Richmond, the best player in existence.

@fro_music

Raphael - Fire on the Sand

Regenerate me into the sun
Fire my soul to the heart of night
As apaches dance orbiting bonfires
where spirits play above the licking crimson heat
And sing of old times and old tides
And children seek reconciliation of the dark
For keeping them awake in fear
And keeping their eyes blind to the world of dim

Carry me please
On your back like you always did
I saw you in the smoke
I know you're watching with ears high
So please
Bear my weight for one last laugh
And let us gallop young
Through fluorescent supermarkets
And public pools
And ghost libraries 5 minutes from closing
Let us tip buckets on the pier
And set free the fisherman's catch
He can eat herbivorous tonight

Take me too
Still cloud
To packed out theatres
Where we can holler the twist ending
And watch the patrons curse
Let us make a day of it
And watch the juvenile sun rise its body above the Pacific
And set to lull sleep over the Atlantic, just once more can we run?
Just once more can we drop ourselves into the ocean of living
And see the Coney Island reflective panels
Warp our faces and warp our mind
Please

...

When I stand there
Without you
No angle in the mirror
Ever warps my expression
Into a smile
So, say yes
Just this last time
While the smoke is still rising
And the fire still dancing
Let us be together
Just one last time
Somewhere beyond
Our own memories

@raphaellove.music

Matcho - Passion

.Passion
I met her when I was thirteen
She seemed to be everything I believed that was good
But not everything I conceived
I should have known not to fill up mystery with fantasy
But I also knew what hasn't been would
and... that..
If I went with her
Then I'd have everything I had always wanted
But you see the more I grew out of childhood
The more I realized that everyone else had a piece of her
But they didn't treat her the way I did
They did things and talked about it
More than how I explored about it
I just wanted to show them how best to bless her
mmmm,
See I was in love with passion
She had me at :   "Let's do this!"

As ambivalent as our relationship
When ever I showed her I was into her
She'd reciprocate me with the same amount of sentiment

I was so into passion that others became envious of our love
Not knowing how they can get their own they'd give me mean mugs

Even though I'd give them fiends love
See on the stream of things to come
They'd be all critical of passion and how she had to stay
They pretend to be my friends just to get her away
But as much as our times became strain
Nothing could break me away from passion
I wrote a poem about her
That I know nobody can match   "Hmmmph!"

Passion, ever since I met you I've been true to the game
Everybody try to spend the weekend with you, but I do you each day
The fact that failure tries to climb you
Bringing issues to stay
And doubt plagues the minds of those that you influence
Bringing you all this pain
And I bet logic does it's own on you
Just to drive you insane

But you see failure doesn't know the roots that you came
Doubt doesn't realise the hoops that you've faced
And logic is ashamed you bring his troops through the rain

So what I'm saying is that passion you are the truest of traits
So this is an appreciation for you doing what you do to just stay

Whenever you are around I put illusion to the grave
The day you leave me is when I intrude my own fate
When I stand to look like all the others
A beautiful disgrace ...

@matcho_makata

Milky Bar Kid - The Cycle

Every revolution produces a new order
Every order creates a new structure
A place to operate within, allowing flow
through limitation.
A channel, path or direction
Without constraints , we can not construct
Motivation is needed to move matter to form
Without tasks to perform we become static
Lost in a sea of opportunity
Language comes from order
To understand is to perceive patterns
To know what to say requires constraints
and restrictions

Limitations mould actions and allow us
To make meaning from what's in reach
We teach the young to imitate and then create
So they can take part in the dance between order and chaos
the dance Is internal, external and eternal
Every order becomes too rigid, too safe
Every revolution produces a new order

@milkybarkidofficial

Shyaire Ganglani - Wigbolt

In dark wooden booths,
we sipped stories,
spilling secrets,
hearts dancing
in metaphors of love,
anecdotes of loss,
fingers trailed desperately
trying to etch our body maps,
scrunched noses and notes,
tucked in fridges and sock drawers,
smoky wood chips on window sills,
lazy naps on foreign trains,
memories linger,
like whispers
etched in the fabric of time,
till the fifth round
someday,
at that corner bar,
with the usual poison,
and far too many choices of bitters.

@hiddenhaikus

Nayomi Senanayake - Home Pt II

I thought I had found a home with her.
Our foreheads kissed, my eyes closed
concentrating on the glow sitting on my diaphragm.
I was wrapped in every shade of green that filtered
her eyes, the freckles dancing across her collarbone.

But soon she found my bones were difficult,
buried under stubborn weeds and lined with thistles,
I was not a safe place to lay down her head.

So I'm tending alone to thorny buds and
examining knobbly bones,
learning how to care for those parts me
that don't seem to deserve any tenderness.

I'm setting words against a page
to feel my breath, placing on the hearth
my scarred bark,
my prickly fears,
my vulnerability scorched.

A home needs love
but to love this ground
lined with my mistakes and
the parts of myself I would rather hide,
seems an impossible task.
A radical act but the only one that makes sense,
my home is me.

Amy - Fuck You Helen

I get it, Helen, I know you're feeling irate
But you found god in your husband's prostate
And I know cancer's scary (for a cancer patient's wife)
But he got it three times and he never fucking died

So fuck you Helen, you're a really shit mum
Cos you clearly made your choice, and you didn't pick your sons
Mattie's full homo ahead, Michael's engaged
Don't know about Jen (but we know she isn't straight)

I know you said you've loved me from the day that I was born
You were in the room - cut my umbilical cord
But I took my bestie to Kevin's birthday
And you wouldn't speak to me
You're like "oh shit, is Amy GAY?" (yes)

So fuck you, Helen you're a really shit gran
Cos you only seem to love me if I'm dating a man
And it's not just me you're hurting or the lesbians and gays
It's every single person LGBTQIA

Stephen tried to tell me you struggled with your decision
I looked him in the face and laughed with derision
If Helen really loved her kids, I think she'd struggle harder
Instead of taking orders from an imaginary father

So fuck you, Helen, for when you voted no
Fuck you for thinking you get to say so
It's not like you'd "gay" marry anyway
So fuck you for thinking you deserve to have a say

Helen, I know you're not here to hear me berate you
But you deserve to know why your granddaughter hates you
See you're so wrapped up in Sky Dad who lives up above you
You can't even see I no longer even love you

So fuck you, Helen, for giving church a hand
To try and get god to get into my pants
Whoever I marry that should be up to me
So tell god to get his hands off my fucking ovaries

See this is where it started, all of our fights
When you decided other people don't deserve human rights
god was your reason to deny this institution
But last time I checked you still believe in evolution

So fuck you, Helen, for god and cherry-picking
Fuck you for bringing god into politicking
Fuck you for saying Jesus was a refugee
When you blame all your problems on the Sudanese

You've known god five years and your children all their lives
But suddenly your best friend is the fucking Transformed Wife
What is up with the backflip on what is right or wrong
Or were you just pretending to accept me all along

So fuck you, Helen, for hating on the gays
Fuck you, Helen, god never said that's ok
Fuck you for thinking I shouldn't fuck women
Fuck you from everyone for what you did to 'em

@terreurnocturne

Thank You

Vibe Union, Ry and Myself (Jason), would like to thank all those who have had a hand in shaping Radio Talk into the event it is today. Whether that be previously or currently, the input and effort spent by everyone will and has always been appreciated.

Radio Bar Fitzroy - @radio_bar

Saskia - @chaupaemisque - Photos

Porsche Jansuwan @takenbyporsche - Photos

Nick - @nickrohanmusic - Guitar

Huich - @huichgoh - Violin

Matt Robb - @mat.robb - Guitar

Nikko - @nikko_morganlowe - Guitar

Nathan - @nathanabbbey - Guitar

Jason - @user.name.unknown.jason - Vibe Union & MC

Ry - @rhath_music - Vibe Union & Sound Engineer

We have to thank our youngest poetry attendee for their contribution of their artwork seen on the front cover of this book.

We also want to show our appreciation to all the poets who contributed:

Ryu
Gerard
Izzy (last name redacted)
Jocelyn
Xlvi Joon
S.T.P
Saskia McKippers
Kelsey Jean
Lane Milburn
Michael Bromberg
Daniel Whimpey
Jaidyn L Attard
Rhath
Beverley
Marcus Graham
Jett
Raphael
Matcho
Antonio
Dilly Dave
Shyaire Ganglani
Nayomi Senanayake
Amy

www.ingramcontent.com/pod-product-compliance
Lightning Source LLC
Chambersburg PA
CBHW070312010526
44107CB00056B/2567